ANTARCTIC AMBUSH

Contents

OXFORD
UNIVERSITY PRESS

My name is **Birdy**, and I'm from future Earth. 2099 to be precise. My world is at risk – a giant asteroid is on a collision course with the planet.

Kalvin Spearhead, head of **END CO** – the most powerful company on Earth – plans to build a giant vortex machine to send people back in time to escape the asteroid. He has assembled a team of human-like robots, **Tick-Tock Men**, to collect seven **Artefacts of Time**. These Artefacts will be used to power his machine.

My gran, **Professor Martin**, is the head scientist at END CO. She has shown me Spearhead's plans; she doesn't think his machine is capable of transporting vast numbers of people. Even if the machine does work, it will have a devastating effect on history: it could change everything! Gran has tried to tell Spearhead, but he won't listen. I decided I had to try to stop him. I have borrowed one of my gran's old-tech time-travel vortex machines – an **Escape Wheel** – and am trying to reach the Artefacts of Time before the Tick-Tock Men do.

Luckily, I'm not alone on my journey. I've met four new friends – **Max**, **Cat**, **Ant** and **Tiger**. They have special watches that can make them shrink to micro-size … which comes in handy when the Tick-Tock Men try to stop us!

Chapter 1: Cold as ice

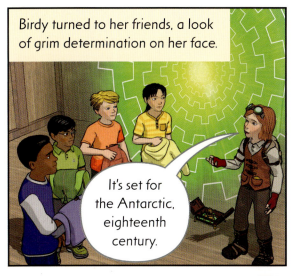

Birdy turned to her friends, a look of grim determination on her face.

It's set for the Antarctic, eighteenth century.

Are you sure you've got the coordinates right?

I ... think so. I've narrowed the parameter settings to zero.

Suddenly nobody felt very confident about entering the vortex.

Honestly guys, it'll be fine.

We just jump on to the ship – the *Resolution* – make sure the sea clock's safe and …

Hang on, did you say the *Resolution*? That was one of Captain Cook's ships!

What are we waiting for? Let's go!

Fingers crossed this works …

Suddenly there was a shimmering light. The smell of ozone filled the air.

Uh oh, this isn't right.

Nooooooo!

The vortex had gone haywire. There was nothing but light and sound, roaring, exploding around them.

Then they began to fall …

They lay breathless for a while, tangled in a heap, then Tiger struggled to his feet.

It's freezing!

Well, at least we know you got us to the right place, Birdy. Is it the right time?

Yep. According to my pocket watch it's the 21ˢᵗ December 1773. Told you there was nothing to worry about.

Hold on, where's Cat?

I thought she was in front of us.

Cat? Cat!

Their faces were pinched raw with the cold. Their teeth were chattering. And they had lost Cat!

It's all my fault. I shouldn't have messed around with the settings on the Escape Wheel.

There's no point thinking like that … Focus: where could Cat have gone?

Birdy's pocket watch is a crucial piece of her time-travel kit. Given to her by her gran for her 10th birthday, it helps her to navigate through time and track other vortex activity. This makes it essential for tracking down Tick-Tock Men.

Time and place navigator: lets Birdy know when and where she has travelled to

Twelve-hour clock: so Birdy's pocket watch can also be used to tell the real time too!

Metal outer case: made of a hard-wearing metal called Neminium

Vortex activity tracker: lets Birdy know if other time vortexes have been opened nearby. Although useful, this feature is not incredibly accurate, so Birdy must also rely on other methods to find Tick-Tock Men.

Hang on a second, does anyone else get the feeling we're being watched?

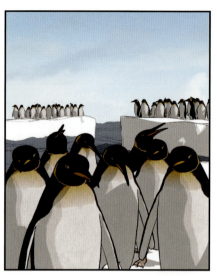

The friends stared out over the ice floes.

They're just penguins. You're being paranoid.

However, somebody else *was* observing the friends …

Stowaways! Lousy, scurvy stowaways.

None of the friends could speak. They were paralyzed with fright.

The presence of the four friends baffled the crew.

Minutes later …

What's all the commotion? Children? Where have you been hiding?

Come on, speak up.

If you don't tell me how you came to be on board then …

Please sir …

We didn't stow away. We …

Max's words evaporated into the air as he realized he couldn't tell the captain the truth. It was too incredible.

Yes, you're right. We stowed away.

9

What made you mention the sea clock?

I was desperate … it just popped out.

Well, next time pop it back in again!

Squabbling won't get us anywhere.

We've got our watches — let's shrink!

And go where exactly?

Good point. We might as well wait for Captain Cook to come and get us.

What about Cat?

She'll be OK.

I hope.

Consumed with worry for their lost friend, they sat in silence, listening to the creak of the rigging and the groan of the wooden hull as the boat rocked on the waves. They waited ...

... And they waited.

Chapter 2: Alone at sea

The *Resolution* was not alone on that frozen sea. Not far away, under the cold, Antarctic sky, there was a second, identical, ship.

Somebody stirred: a lone, lost figure.

Max? Tiger? Ant?

Birdy?

Where is everybody?

I don't like this. I don't like it one bit.

Cat's teeth began to chatter. She had never felt so cold. The chill bit into her bones.

Cat flipped open the screen on her watch. With frozen fingers, she activated her tracker.

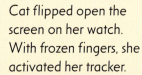

They're close.

Hello?

Her lone voice was lost to the whistling wind

Anyone?

I guess I'll try below deck.

Anyone here?

No crew. The ship's deserted.

And what happened to my friends?

Cat thought she was alone, but something was stirring nearby …

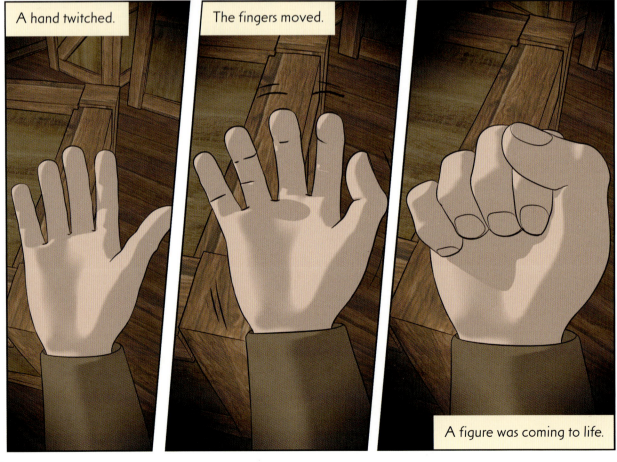

A hand twitched.

The fingers moved.

A figure was coming to life.

Cat backed away, heart slamming in her chest.

More figures emerged from the gloom.

Chapter 3: Ship ahoy!

If Captain Cook isn't coming to get us, then we'll just have to go and find him. We've wasted enough time.

At last! Some action!

They turned their watches two notches and pressed the button to shrink.

Blip, Blip, Blip ...

Where now?

They grew back to normal size and crept back up to the main deck.

Let's try through there ...

Anything?

To starboard!

What are they looking at?

Sssshhhh.

What can you see?

Ship ahoy!

Another ship? This far south in the Antarctic?

How did you escape from the brig?

Captain, before you deal with them, there is something you have to see.

It's a ship, sir. The name on the side reads *Resolution*!

Impossible!

The other ship was getting ever closer.

Are you thinking what I'm thinking?

Err, Captain …

What is it?

It's about that ship …

But there was no time for Birdy to explain.

Captain! There's something else …

Captain, there are even more of them.

It's your sea clock they're after. We tried to tell you earlier.

Yeah, before you locked us up!

What do these machines want with my timepiece?

They are collecting important clocks. Your sea clock is more valuable than you realize.

The Tick-Tock ship no longer looked deserted, and it was closing in on the real *Resolution*. Fast!

Chapter 4: Up the rigging

A few minutes earlier …

Uh oh.

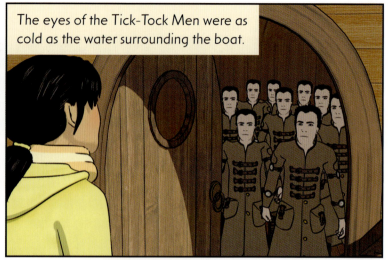

The eyes of the Tick-Tock Men were as cold as the water surrounding the boat.

Where can I hide?

Get back!

OK, here goes nothing.

Where are my friends when I need them?

They don't seem to be on the ship, but they're close. So where are they?

Another ship!

The others must be on it!

Cat tried to attract the attention of the crew of the *Resolution*.

Aaaaaargh!

It's a young girl!

Let me see!

It's Cat! And that Tick-Tock Man is just behind her!

We've got to do something.

That isn't our only problem!

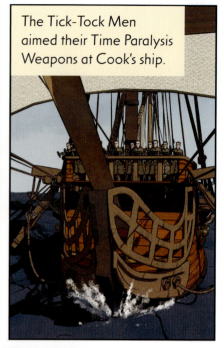

The Tick-Tock Men aimed their Time Paralysis Weapons at Cook's ship.

You've got to help Cat! Use your Caliber Glove!

They're a hundred metres away. They're out of range.

How close do you need to be?

Another ten metres, maybe?

The Tick-Tock ship continued to close on the *Resolution*. It was nearly in range.

But Birdy had only immobilized one Tick-Tock Man …

What's happening?

Simply put, he's been paralyzed. The effects will wear off … eventually.

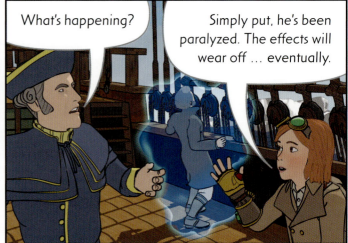

Then we're as good as dead!

Get back everyone!

If the Tick-Tock Men kept paralyzing the crew, there would be nobody to sail the ship …

… the two vessels would crash.

Can I help?

Not unless you can steer that other ship out of the way!

The two mighty ships were minutes away from a catastrophic collision.

Somebody's got to do something …

… and it looks like it's down to me.

I need to get to that wheel.

Here goes nothing …

Taking a deep breath, Cat launched herself into mid-air, hurtling towards the deck.

Yeehaaaaaa!

Geronimo!

She's reckless.

She's a hero.

Come on, Cat, you can do it!

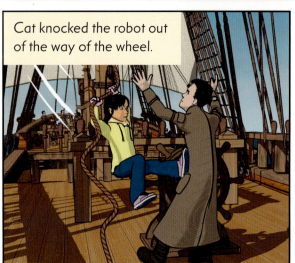

Cat knocked the robot out of the way of the wheel.

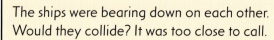

The ships were bearing down on each other. Would they collide? It was too close to call.

Cat desperately strained against the pull of the wheel.

She did it. A mere child guided that vast ship away from us.

Go, Cat!

Captain Cook looked at the friends with new-found respect.

Uh oh!

Can you jump over to us now, Cat?

Geronimo! AGAIN!

I think I'm getting the hang of this rope swinging!

You saved the ship, young lady.

It was nothing.

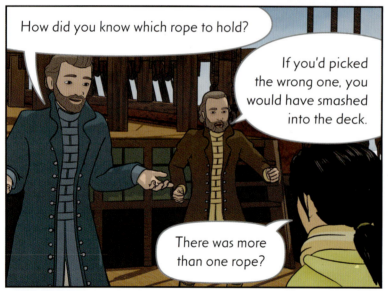

How did you know which rope to hold?

If you'd picked the wrong one, you would have smashed into the deck.

There was more than one rope?

I think I need to sit down.

I'm afraid it isn't over yet.

Max is right. The ship is coming round again — but this time we've got no allies on board!

There was no time to take a breath before the second attack was underway.

The Tick-Tock ship was getting nearer and nearer, its crew determined to obtain Captain Cook's sea clock.

They're going to fire again!

Protect the sea clock …

You'll find it on the table in my cabin …

Captain!

Captain Cook was frozen, just like one of the icebergs nearby.

Shrink!

For Captain Cook and his crew, it was too late. Only the five friends could save the *Resolution* now.

Danger loomed ever closer …

Ant, Birdy, get the sea clock … We'll return to normal size and steer the ship.

Iceberg ahead!

All together … TURN!

We did it!

Only just.

Tick-Tock Men preparing to board!

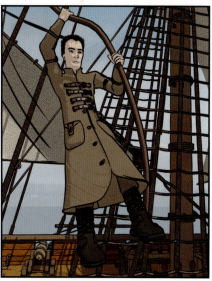

Get it, somebody!

The sea clock was lost forever beneath the thirsty waves.

They're giving up.

They must sense the sea clock's lost.

It's my fault it's gone.

At least the Tick-Tock Men don't have it either.

Ant's right. We stopped them from taking it.

So in a way we've won?

Don't speak too soon.

The Tick-Tock ship started to turn again.

Don't they ever give up?

They're planning to sink us ...

... so we can't stop them from getting the next Artefact of Time?

Exactly. Well, two can play that game! Help me out here.

I'll get this set up just in case ...

Don't ... worry ... we'll ... make ... it ...

Who would lose their nerve first, the five friends or the Tick-Tock Men?

They're turning!

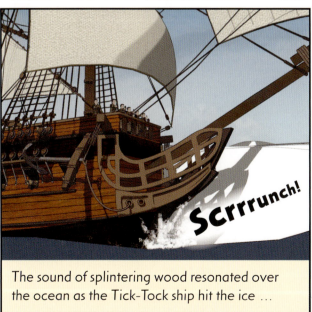

Scrrrunch!

The sound of splintering wood resonated over the ocean as the Tick-Tock ship hit the ice …

That will slow them down.

It might delay them, but it won't stop them forever.

No, but it should give us a bit of time. Birdy, can you get us out of here?

Just a minute.

All set.

No more malfunctions?

I've changed the settings.

It should work properly.

SHOULD?

One by one the friends stepped into the vortex …

As the effects of the Time Paralysis Weapon wore off, Captain Cook and his crew started to move again.

Where are the children?

Children? I don't know what you mean. The cold has muddled your senses.

But …

Not a word must pass your lips about what happened here today. Our voyage must continue. Understand?

Yes, Captain!

I was right to hide the clock safely away. What a relief it is only my pocket watch that is gone and not the sea clock.

Captain James Cook was born on 27th October 1728, in the village of Marton, near Middlesbrough. On 1st August 1768, Captain Cook undertook his first voyage of discovery aboard the *Endeavour*, visiting Australia and New Zealand.

On 13th July 1772, Captain Cook's second voyage began aboard the *Resolution*. He crossed the Antarctic Circle for the first time in history and explored the South Seas. He took a new invention, a sea clock, with him on this journey for testing. The sea clock had been designed by the English clockmaker John Harrison and aimed to solve a problem sailors had encountered for a long time – accurately fixing their location. Captain Cook took a copy of Harrison's clock made by another clockmaker, Larcum Kendall. Even though it was a copy, it still took three years to make! Captain Cook was so pleased with the clock's performance that he took it on his next journey, too.

On 12th July 1776, Captain Cook began his third and final voyage of discovery, taking him to Hawaii, Tahiti, New Zealand, America, Canada and other destinations. On 14th February 1779, Cook died in a confrontation with armed warriors in Hawaii.